The City of Missing People

PIOTR
GAWELKO

THE
CITY
OF
MISSING
PEOPLE

STANDBY & GO

Copyright © 2014 by Piotr Z. Gawelko.
All rights reserved. Except for brief passages quoted in a newspaper, magazine, radio, or television review, no part of this book may be reproduced in any form or by any means, electronic or mechanical, including photocopying and recording, or by any information storage and retrieval, without permission in writing from the Publisher.
Manufactured In the United States of America.

ISBN: 978-1-939029-14-0

Acknowledgments

The Publisher here records his thanks;
Editing by David Audun.
Design and Typography by Aneta Swierzko
Cover Photo by Gabriel Oshen
Cover Design by Asia Borycka
Proof Reading by Susan Bickerstaff

FIRST EDITION

Published by: STANDBY & GO
cityofmissingpeople@gmail.com

CONTENTS

PIKA AND OCEAN	1
SUSPENSION BRIDGE	2
CHAMOMILE BAR	3
ESCAPE OF PIKA	5
THE BRICK	7
MIDNIGHT EXPRESS	9
THE MIRROR	11
INTERFERENCE PATTERN	13
ATTICS	14
PIKA	16
SCRAP PEOPLE	17
SECLUSION	19
MONSTER IN NEW YORK	21
PIKA AND END OF THE WORLD	23
ONCE I SAW IN FITFUL FILM	25
HEAVEN DAY: 28	30
PIKA AND GOD	32
CONTRA EVOLUTION 1	34
THE RIVER	35
PIKA AND STORK	37
REAPPEARANCE	39
ROMANTICISM	40
MISCONCEPTION	42
THE CITY OF MISSING PEOPLE	46
RETURN OF PIKA	48
THAT STUPID LOVE	50
THE ANTS	51
W KRUZLOWEJ	52
NEVER MIND CORNER	54

*For my Mother and my Father, my Brother,
my Family, my Friends and my Strangers.*

PIKA AND OCEAN

She wants to be the ocean
and
playing the dark land,
just like that.

Tired
of cheap green,
of menthol,
of submarine cadres,
making herself soft for iron ships
and available
for confrontations with the pirates.

There will be no mercy
this time,
trip
to the thunder
of some association.

SUSPENSION BRIDGE

neatly pulled, yellowed,
yellowed ropes, damned rocks,
cellophane river falls from
the table of the woods,
tightrope walker,
that
is pierced through with it -
spear of barbaric warrior with beard,
who misses the point and ends
somewhere besides,

black bear's breath rises over
an absurd neck,
devours entire suspension bridge
and now,
moves grotesquely,
with arms stretched forward,
with eyes on half,
whining something foreign -
any resemblance… with any reality,
purely
orange of fortuity.

CHAMOMILE BAR

There is an old Willow from which
the Bar is coming out.
Ill advised is anyone who comes,
who comes across, who comes too close
to the Chamomile Bar.

It is somewhere, who knows?
It is where the summer lazily buzzes
and time is determined
by the wheel of a peasant's wagon,
rambling toward the cliff,
rendering it into the dust,
into some sacred speech.

I hit the first infusion:
impulse went…
Unfailingly comforted
I flush my own splendor and minimize
my gravitation.
I walk to the picture hanging on a wall…
It is a reconstruction of a famous painting;
that's *Pere Tanguy,* invariably touched,
overall no reaction to my teasing.
Goodbye Father. I'll be back.

Second infusion:
impulse went…

I talk with bees.
Apparently flowers are extraordinarily
sweet this year and the Queen
is getting married again,
"- what a whore"- bees laugh, but
in the hive views are divided.
Some turning blind, black, sparkling eyes,
imagining to be in her position,
buzz, buzz…
What a departure.
Making love on the viscous honeycombs
in the Royal Bedroom,
buzz…

Third infusion:
impulse went…
The most bittersweet and marvellous.
I am Chamomile.
Insubordinate , Chamomile youngster;
roaming the bar, playing games with the guests,
being shown the back door
which, eventually, I open
coming to the beyond of
any recognition.

ESCAPE OF PIKA

Fact:
she took her orange purse
with
three shiny pennies,
her ping-pong ball,
her mascot Dennis,
and
invitation for the Grammy's.

How sad it is!

Fact:
she likes wine…
so maybe a Vineyard and
that guy with a destiny?

Not here.

My neighbor's pool
keeps cooling
the panicky movement
inside me.

Fact:
She left a letter.
"What a day…
Miles away and not to be found!

I am where I am,
watering cucumbers,
as the cows
come back
to the morning barn.
Not sure of tomorrow,
happy…
Why?
I had enough, I had
enough!"

Pika has been gone. Gone!
I ask mushroom and sparrow;
has she been seen?
And before I finish asking,
they have also disappeared.

THE BRICK

Muggy, sultry spirit,
a ghost in the lighthouse.

White fangs,
pale face, fishy eyes
enslaving,
speaking in pearly paragraphs
and screaming, rips
brocaded, as
dry paper into shreds:
deadly kiss.

Falling, dimensionally, starfish,
my love.

August blinked, blinking carousel,
like an old slut;
attracting, enticing, seductive alcohol,
wrapping in a cocoon
its unhinged shapes,
misty flesh,
feeding rats, cats
and pigeons from the city hall.

Glass. Glass.
The window moves.
The window is breathing.

He jumped from the lighthouse
into November night,
because his mournful lover
proceeded to sea
and did not come back…

Nowadays, in its rough breast,
striking,
striking,
striking waves, the curious,
a curious water…

MIDNIGHT EXPRESS

Midnight express,
expedited in mist, in the bliss of plumes,
seemingly dry,
such a frost on the sapphires and
fails to keep sight of
the participation of growing warmth.

The styrofoam pieces,
years down the corridors,
every so often force open,
spins,
so as it might turn to
the ebb,
upon a voyage to the unknown.

Found:
pretends silly.
Throws octopus' arms
around
and later
hangs itself in nearby park.

Or else.

Just in case, if found,
resting on a stone
in open field,

dispels like all the scarves, that
humming lullabies, lullabies and
mysterious tracks under
the train.

MIDNIGHT EXPRESS

Midnight express,
expedited in mist, in the bliss of plumes,
seemingly dry,
such a frost on the sapphires and
fails to keep sight of
the participation of growing warmth.

The styrofoam pieces,
years down the corridors,
every so often force open,
spins,
so as it might turn to
the ebb,
upon a voyage to the unknown.

Found:
pretends silly.
Throws octopus' arms
around
and later
hangs itself in nearby park.

Or else.

Just in case, if found,
resting on a stone
in open field,

dispels like all the scarves, that
humming lullabies, lullabies and
mysterious tracks under
the train.

THE MIRROR

1.
On the other side of the mirror
I stand.
Unmatchable,
someone I know,
someone I want to be,
but I don't know how.

Scary room with a scary shape,
iron door and a barrel
in the middle.

Scaring hopeless streets
like homicide in the broken,
baking factory.
Why are you taking me away from mine?
If this is only a game…you win.
I don't want to play anymore.
Hurts like thousand knives in my heart,
when what is killing me
is keeping me alive.

2.
The trees are dancing through the sky,
they want to be the rain
and hitting the ground like that.

On the other side of the mirror,
the trees are coming down like rain
and the rain is growing up like the trees.

INTERFERENCE PATTERN

Naturally, *Porto!*
Straight from the source,
under the edge monologues,
                shame at table.
Murmurs, whispers, taps,
            hidden
              spiteful coincidences,
imperialistic pigs,   squeal and squeal
in the barn of their minds.
Distorted time-
ing.
            Transformed reality?
Must not be… how would I know?
That microcosm,
      muffled   in chains,
but,   freer than Tiger River,
supposedly   so little meaning
    and all for show,
      ranging from Icarus at every moment,
car through its interrupted confession.
                    But,
what an impact on colony of Paramecium caudatum!
What a rumor in a puddle…
        Rippling through folks   that,
            coercive landing, that God
has been losing   reminiscences…

ATTICS

Among us… Attics.
Dirt roads that lead to them,
bridges that run away
suddenly…
Before the handle goes down,
before the lips touch the trophy.

Among us… Attics.
Closed chapters.
Inhabited by negatives of our bodies,
trivially solidified
in black and white poses.
Not looking for applause,
nor
to speak.

Drought on ropes ever unspoken words,
as tablecloths,
after all these bloody five o'clock tea parties
with the milky way in the background.

Hollow arms fall into… the Attics,
the same ones that took you then,
neglecting time you dissolve again,
pleasure which is comparable
to the dust.

Mock of those, who have carried the torch
to mark the end of the era.
There is no end…fool
and Attics are precocious.

PIKA

No one whatsoever,
is more clever,
than Pika.

Asian pill with no refill;
and
all you can have is nothing
wrapped in her eyes;
and
all you can take from her
is her execution.

Pika is from Brooklyn
or is she from the dunes?
Some day God will smoke grass
in her backyard,
among all the Bamboo.
That comes next; it comes
kind of soon.

Smokey and Walter because of Cherry…
They're dancing together.
Cherry is kissing Pika,
Pika is going to sleep,
pretty
and dreamless.

SCRAP PEOPLE

they are heralds of a brand new day,
certainly
part of its emergence,

dressed in gray,
bouncing
in a pale
of which
yanking someone's junk,
taking it as it's granted,
sniffing for copper,
up to their knees in mirrors,
anything exchangeable goes;

lamps, televisions, shoes,
boxes for crickets,
personal and generally accessible
ups and bankruptcies of hearts,
tracks, electrical pipes, tubs,
blended wire for worlds,
but also worthless and naive objects,
those that we want,
just because.

I don't care
for them more
than for wild cats:

without a scrap of thought,
that maybe, that maybe,
that by chance, that is Lord.

SECLUSION

Without excuse, without price,
sneaking out of definitions,
smooth as death is my seclusion.

Like Siamese sisters; two heads- one body
has grown to love one.
Two ships shattered by branches of clouds,
one destination.

Then,
the "Breeze" hotel.
Its ironic name
deprives me
of the remaining delusions,
shredding my nerves.

I paid for it what I had
at hand:
sleepless nights, daily ambivalence…
I still smell the fresh paint
and I hear the voice of the Master.
My Dear burial,
garden of nothingness, or
nameless city…

Again;
Here and there dysfunction of lamp;

lighting up
when I'm trying to turn it off, and
slowly dis-abling
when I want it on.

Over again;

I'm getting into a carriage,
that never comes,
pushing horses ridden in a coma,
to catch performance in nonexistent theatre,
which, unwittingly, floats on the water.

MONSTER IN NEW YORK

Bundled alleyways- nervous system.
Subway map- blood circulation.
Skin- urban design.
Heart- Metropolitan Opera.
Eye
- pond in Central Park, but also;
every drip of every sink, every squirt of
every faucet.

On a daily basis,
however,
he is taking the human figure.
Blending well with the crowd,
in his bullet proof slacks,
in his bowler hat,
regardless of mood,
always elegant and flawless.

[Coins clank]

What is he and where is he come from?
We don't know, ah… we don't know.

Hanging out
in cafes and bars,
saluting to the strangers,
asking them about their labile being

with surprising lightness,
contemplating the weather,
throwing money on the arts,
then leaving it,
wherever.

[Cock crow and waves crashing]

Blinded by its brilliance, we can't find the treasure
whose false countenance puts us in the trance.

In general,
a good Monster,
only at times
continually kindness bores him
and then he is doing the wrong;
pulling out the plugs
in public,
pulling out of the pyramid
that apple,
whose absence will take
its solid,
undivided life story.

PIKA AND END OF THE WORLD

No way.

Storm of asymmetric stars.
Too late for forgiveness.
Too late for confession.
Too late for shopping.
Everyone, at different direction.
Four crazy horses knowing
no time is left.

Fire for those
who never were
late.
Fire for those
who never were
confused.
Fire for those
who never were
disappointed.
Fire for those
who never were
pierced by doubt.

Fire!

Pika wrinkles her mouth,
she looks into the distance

and not for a second
stops peeling potatoes.

ONCE I SAW IN FITFUL FILM

A man just left the building
thinking he looks fabulous
in his pomegranate suit,
but loses a glove at first
posh corner.
Someone, somewhere
On the Upper West Side complains
the Venti Mocha is missing the extra shot,
just like yesterday
in Tribeca,
the curtain is going up.

Tomorrow is in a cloakroom
playing Russian Roulette,
the hotdog vendor is
rolling his eyes,
enshrined Madonnas,
dressed up to their teeth, fulfilling
supplications
with a shrug of the shoulders.
Explosion
of laughter on occasion,
(although all that is human is alien to them)
tomorrow's revolver falls like a last leaf,
soundlessly, no witnesses,
as if nothing had been dared.

The man who just hijacked the plane
pressing the wrong button in the cockpit,
the voice cracking over
the air controllers pink headset:

"…we have some planes…
"… just stay quiet…and you'll be okay…
"…we are returning to the airport…"

Filled with pulsating fear
the hunted bird rushes over
the Hudson River, beside Manhattan Island.
Low, way too low.
Amazed skyscrapers bend sideways,
concerned elevators whose eyelids
carrying in cabins anxiety and wine.

8:45…AM
Flight 11 cuts into windpipe of Northern Giraffe.
All the animals in our jungle
lift their heads and tails
and all the sirens in reserved boxes
begin to howl their siren song
(blockbuster of terminating summer):
"Oh my God".

The CNN dude keeps babbling,
reporting life from the other side,
heavy camcorder's multicolor lenses,
enter areas where fragile eyes do not.
Alleging we have an accident,
(closes in parentheses- *raging fire*),

the rescue operation continues
deoxidizing number of the victims.

The more, the better occasion
of course
to call to friends far and abroad,
the more dramatic the easier
to talk to neighbors from ground zero.

9:03...AM
Flight 175 from nowhere
to the screen of my television,
exquisite, subtly constructed
Dragon-fly sticks into
membrane of Southern Giraffe.

And silence.
The same silence that fills the fraction before death.
(I know because I have died once already)
Next there are no more questions in mind,
as afterward it all turns out
child's play or hell.

In dread of an attack on my person and kingdom,
I hide in the profundity of my top drawer,
I extend my feelers casually but in time
and I set my decoy on the balcony of Wall Street.

An old Jew prays on his knees,
the only constant element on the margin,
all the rest are running waywardly
and speaktoselfily doomed.

How clever the footprints,
like they don't belong to anybody,
jumping out of windows,
going down like folding chairs,
to be captured by fallen angels
in the last rapture
of world become unbearable.

Burning giraffes in different states of chaos,
suffocating panic breaks measurements of all,
no clue who I am,
I join the rats and feel loved.

9:59..Am
The agony of the Northern
is ending now,
like an express train going on vertical track,
taking passengers to land of eternal hunt,
together with those who are not.

With the power of a hundred and ten floors,
plunging into after battle landscapes,
like mad dogs let off the chain,
talking block after block,
the black cloud in its ignorance,

Covering the alleys in an eiderdown of dust,
like a quilt-monster on decadent catwalk,
crawls out into my city,
jolting obscurity on my ratty temple.

Then we off in leaps and bounds,
entire group, rigid but blurred,
I spew debris from my snout,
repeatedly, and
somehow
I start
to think about spring…

The Southern antenna catches a short signal.
"Do to this…"
It is 10:28…
AM.

HEAVEN DAY: 28

The rustle of beetles
is simply delightful
and the light
reflected off their scales
floods the room
in which I'm the middle.
I am progressively resigning
from human habits;
as of yesterday
I don't look back
- no point.
Followed by
I give up dreams coming true,
such is the mundane…and
nothing
like the Palace!
Snow on the mountains.
Its gates
emerge,
omitting a sense of distance,
finishing with posters
at all the premiers,
played out on mainstage.
Be added:
I am going on an excursion
of the boundaries of the kingdom.
Professedly, "it is out of the sight",

Grandma said, "it is too much",
well,
she has always been old-fashioned
and not always right.

PIKA AND GOD

- Hi God!

- Hi Pika, what's up?

- I'm devastica...For million years,
for a great heaven of dimmed deers,
some don't know
that You are for real, that I am for real!

- Well, sucks to be them.
Besides;
The Almighty went out alone
that's why I'm little worried,
hell knows what he's gonna do, but
that is a different story.

What do you want?

- I know is quite insane, but,
let me be born again,
delete my soul,
pronounce me deceased,
my star has expired
in mist...I insist!

- I made you to be a Pika...
I know the best,

I know the best;
where is the west, where is the east,
where…sleeps the beast.
Goodbye.

- Master? Master?

- Dear?

CONTRA EVOLUTION 1

strangely enough, the Fish is not
even close to coming out of the fucking sea,
since the dawn the paws did not sprout,
no embryo of a leg has been detected,
no voice has been heard,
strangely enough,
we… the fish, are not going anywhere,
we are just fine, here, in the water;
strangely enough, I think, and,
with no nucleus of wing,
I am going to welcome upcoming winter.

THE RIVER

Another parade, look!
-lion seal!
Floats like a log,
look!
Is going for astonished stones,
semi-wet, half-death,
sentinels of infinite subsidence.

In the village…they said,
that if suitably bribed
the stones may tell
some legends.
Suppose I'm fortunate to hear
the great mystery. Now,
I'm seriously concerned.

I sold all I had,
the only saleable now,
my body,
shrouded in black tulle;
I dumped all the gold in the river and
I sat down in the depths
ready for disclosure.

Honing the stone in place,
cold and slimy,
makes me

meander like a loach,
makes me
sink into abdomen of branches,
flooding my lungs with
nectar of white lilies,
instantly drifting away,
my distress.

The moss bristled on the river's head.
All the water subsided.
Angelic voice suddenly sings:

Crossing the barrier of
dilapidated, enforced delusions,
seed,
thrown on that morning plowed escarpment
will grow in your gathered footprints.
Some will have less to go to;
where the bones and craniums
in gloomy silence, and only
the Crow, as a watchmen,
throws at them, short, cutting glances
and caws.
But,
some will grow wildly...
in the splendour:
jumping on, soaring from the lianas,
doing wonders,
under these prodigious leaves.

PIKA AND STORK

At down of golden linens,
only *you* turn around pictures
like that.

Tuesday's afternoon hydrophobia
of yours,
variable like halo
and only traces on the hay…

Where have you been walking?

Where have you taken those,
attached to the shower curtain,
phantom shots from, and why
is the Stork here?

Where have you been walking?

At down of golden linens
Pika is getting ready.
She's putting on
this stunning,
woven of fogs and lights,
necklace…

Bad princess
does not answer any questions,

rotates and vanishes
into the sleeve.

Which paths have you trampled, honey,
where have you been walking?

REAPPEARANCE

So you are.
Almost the same,
but not the same.
You appeared even stronger.
How could I reject you?

Avalanche of my
waiting
slides
and fills me to
the brim.
The seemingly mild,
but... it is so
not.

[Clock chimes]

I flow out of my secretariat,
through an aviary,
via burdened microcircuits
of my contradictions.
The passion flower,
(on which sat the glow-worm)
shuddered and opened,
closed and opened and closed
and opened.

ROMANTICISM

It is indeed, precisely, what
they both ever wanted…
Whether they only could be
someone else, or,
perhaps,
even anybody else.

Dark trees hang into the pond,
already.
Noise ratio of grass, intersects his breath,
from it's every blade.
Is that you?
He hears gallop coming from the hills.
He coverhands his face and
he looks down.
And the earth beneath parts.
And the thunderclap goes twice.
His every division starts to seek for relief,
like a vole,
who wants to enter the mink.

At first;
he just walks around him,
walks and looks at him,
as one is the greatest,
as one is never going to stop being,
like

here and now
is where all begins and ends.

Stony dowries of lions from nearby courtyards
come to life and observe the meadow, on which
is happening, on which the prophecy is fulfilling:

The King is crowning the Groom.
The Groom is crowning the King.

MISCONCEPTION

How do you know?
You just got here.
Prologue?
No,
no, you will be
better off.
Kill
all the phenomena of the world,
of nature and the elements.
One-eyed cat
will point the path,
its banks will embrace you
dispassionately.
Fade of beauty,
cold axe,
four blows precisely.

Befuddled like a poet in manufacture,
I am cutting the stools out of sheetrock
and I am arranging them on the conveyor belt,
which in my opinion
is not going
where they say it does.
I must be careful of my powerful wings,
that they not get into all,
all these toothed wheels,
transmissions and pistons.

Angels for example,
seem not to give a damn about it.
They smoke tobacco and drink vodka on the rocks,
as if the aura that is piercing them
isn't enough for stupefaction.

Don'tknowers…

Highly improvised.

Manifestation of a free mind.

Don't let them tempt you.
Luxury
of their youthful hips
gushes circumstantially
in the recesses of indistinct archways.
Where sunset is only a blur
and sunrise appears sluttier than
a cowhide purse
at the everyday- New Eve Party.
Behind you, all scatters,
like a quartz
in the middle of
cascade,
in the center of attending shadows,
ready to go.

I have Them all
cornered and stoned,
while the Collector
is making some odd audio files…

unsuspecting
from behind his bushy eyebrows, and
is stacking vacant bottles by colors,
like
abandoned smokestacks.

Do it, now!

Murder
the inflatable, loving
in common,
riffraff and gods:

s u p e r f i c i a l i t y.

There is cleanness contained in the ordinary,
… parapeted-cities in one breath.
Its decalcomania is more effective on
white-wet refrigerators
in old, dingy kitchens.

 I just
got the head to sleep,
that is filming kaleidoscopes,
stained-glass saints' triangular faces,
prior to any life.

I have
just seeped into the furrows,
explanation is not necessary
and I am getting out of here,
certainly not staying.

*Yet the stones
on my earthworks
bloom out of the blue,
and my figure thins
to the degree
of dew.*

THE CITY OF MISSING PEOPLE

Grim tenements, grayish,
rapid strides for which no one
is waiting.
No electricity.
Water.
Trains: arrivals
only.
Souvenirs; brimmed hats, shades
and slides
available online
only.
Lanterns; just are,
only.
Gazettes;
back and forth
read by
wind,
only.
Here;
reigns
an eternal evening.
Here;
no one wants to know others
and
no one stares at others.

Here;
no one can tell,
what it takes to get
a dorm
in
the city
of missing people.

RETURN OF PIKA

Return of Pika
was not easy;
day was
breezy,
she was
dizzy,
alone,
at the end of the bus.

Return of Pika is
not sporadic.
She lost her magic
while she was
gone.

Today is the day.
Pika and I are blown away,
making tea for the night.

She so unique,
even now when she's
down.
Pika's tears are
drowning my heart.

Now, I am listening to
Radio Moscow;

Pika is back home, playing
sticks with R2D-2.

The air pressure
is
satisfactory.

THAT STUPID LOVE

Time does not cure
my wounds.
On the contrary,
this love
builds up
a castle,
overgrown with ivy,
builds up a hanging
garden… where
is walking and resting.

Day and night, comes with
                    "new ideas",
with which I must
somehow cope…

THE ANTS

I must not

get rid of these ants

which construct a highway

in my kitchen.

I don't care much about any other ants,

but,

these are my ants

and

I will make sure, that

they are happy.

I must help them

and

I must keep loving them.

(catching myself giving them sugar multiple times).

W KRUZLOWEJ

In Kruzlowa
from one end to the other,
in ensorcelled groves, a tower
sinks darkly into itself.

Noon heat beats the concrete,
ferns scream…
Momentarily interrupting falling shadows,
an inarticulate sigh
hangs in the hollow. How,
to my wonder, how
can it have so blasted the earth?

And carrying up and up,
thicket and heather growing,
and lupine climbing to heaven;
as anyone from their cotton-candy house
would wail;
"O fouled earth!" Now
no one remembers the tower,
mere dust in strata,
merely a Clearing in the night,
where strange things happen,
decipherable to none.
And then;
the shaking, the freaking shaking,
what unseen steadily scalps the seen,

pounding with dull rhythm, relentless rhythm.
As centrifuged robes in slow motion,
this heartless Dervish dancing,
turning like a mill of drunken thieves,
an evil sorcerer scoring hearts.
No searching for answers now;
and why?
Having gone nearly to the end of existence,
blindly splitting universes,
stiffening to enclosing darkness.
And then:

White walls…in three parts;
behind me (which I can't see)
there should be a door.
Making four: a room, and with a window.
Surely I'm lying down,
the ceiling is ahead of me,
and as if lying on it,
the radiant drip solution.
I could swear
from each bead sliding down
my blood cools,
drip, by drip, by drip;
and feeling better, and better, and…
"He's coming back", nurses whisper,
turning toward a cat.
"Doctor"…cat murmurs,
"He's back."

(trans. D.A.)

NEVER MIND CORNER

I'm blind but I see colors.
I see black like my past, and white,
but the rest of them are questionable.
I'm deaf but I hear voices all the time.
They try to convince me to dance with them
above and over imaginary precipices.
But I'm not stupid!
I cannot taste,
that's right, mud is no different from tomato,
except for their consistency.
I don't have a sense of smell,
but the blossom of the apple tree
I can catch
even without my tremulous hands.

Thank you to my Mentor; DAVID AUDUN for everything.

PIOTR GAWELKO was born 1976 in Rybnik, Poland. As a child he was "content to know the world ended at the east side of a stone wall in Berlin." He studied forestry at the Technikum Lesne in Brynek, and went for the first time to Paris, ending contentment. After graduating he studied archeology at the University of Warsaw. He is now living in New York.

Made in the USA
Middletown, DE
18 May 2025

75674891R00043